I0159016

Confidently Maturing in Professionalism

Practical Advice Helping You Mature Two Pages at a Time

Lisa A. Bracy

Copyright © 2018 Lisa A. Bracy

All rights reserved.

ISBN:0-9998650-0-5
ISBN-13: 978-0-9998650-0-2

DEDICATION

To Lexi and James, the next generation to get out there
and take on the world.

CONTENTS

This Page Was Intentionally Left Blank

ACKNOWLEDGMENTS

First and foremost, I am thankful to God for the abundance of blessings that he has bestowed upon me. To my husband, my soulmate Jermaine, thank you for always being so loving, patient and supportive. Your positive personality is such an inspiration, I love you <u>times infinity</u>—**YOU LOSE.**

To my parents, thank you for raising me to be the woman I am today, and for always giving your kids your absolute best. To my brother, thank you for always telling me "you got this" regardless of the journey I am on. To my children, thank you for filling our home with laughter, joy, and creativity.

To my Michelle, 20 years later and you are still there for it all. Thank you for being so loving, for listening, and for believing in me. Thank you for the laughs, that only you and I seem to understand. I love you so much, God has amazing things in store for you!

To my Katerina, no matter the distance you always brighten my day. Thank you for being there. You are a wonderful friend and I love you so much!
To Melinda and Ashes, "hey thanks" for always reading my books and encouraging me to continue. For being silly with me and telling me "Lisa, you are driving me crazy" or "Lisa, you can do it!"

I love you all, may God bless you abundantly today and always. Here's to the first of many books!

A NOTE TO THE READER

One may wonder why each topic of this book is written as a two page read. It is simple. I know something for a fact, we are all busy people. We are all trying to make the most of our day, squeezing every possible minute out of the day to be faster, stronger, or simply a better person. This even applies to our "lazy days," where we sit and say, "I just need five more minutes of silence, television, or sleep."

I get it, I want all of that too. I understand busy. I am a full time employee, wife, mother, student, teacher and writer. I would love to have resources that take hardly any time at all to read but are jam packed with content that makes me say, "that two minutes was worth my time." I want to walk away from information and feel like I truly learned something from it.

Have you seen those growth charts for little kids? Parents buy these for nurseries, daycares for classrooms, and doctors' offices for tracking growth. I am looking at life as a journey up the growth chart, and have decided that the chart does not end until we breathe our last breath. Embrace learning and growth confidently with everything in you.

May this book help you on your journey to confidently maturing.

1
APPEARANCE

My son rushed into the bedroom announcing that he was ready to go. There were only a few problems with that: his jeans looked like a cow had chewed on them through the night, his shirt was half tucked in and he picked perhaps the muddiest shoes possible to leave the house in. Not exactly, what I envisioned for a holiday performance.

I have heard people say that appearance doesn't matter, but let me be blunt: in a professional environment, it does matter. Truth be told there are a lot of judgmental people in the world. I have sat in on job interviews with people about whom owners and managers have made comments such as, "Why would I hire someone to represent my business looking like that?" or, "What kind of effort will they make for my business if they put so little effort into caring for themselves today?" Harsh? Perhaps, but I am not going to sugar coat things for you.

While I understand that every business has its own tendencies toward certain types of attire, there are some simple to-do's that can change not only how others view you, but how you view yourself. You can feel better and more confident in who you are by following a few simple "rules." Some things may seem like basic common sense, but we have all had different life experiences and upbringings, so read on with a bit of grace.

How to achieve a professional look?

SELF CARE
*Smile
*Be confident-even if you are nervous
*Speak clearly and loudly (but not too loud)
*Shower or wash up
*Comb or style hair including facial hair
(if applicable)

PROFESSIONAL ATTIRE
*Wear clean clothing and shoes
*Iron clothing or use a wrinkle release product (in a pinch)
*Be aware of the company dress code and follow it
*Dress modestly (this is always your safest bet)
*Do not wear attire with possibly offensive language or connotations
*Consider adding a blazer or scarf
*Use perfumes, colognes or strong smelling deodorants minimally (others may have allergies to certain products or scents)
*Keep jewelry or accessories to a minimum
*Avoid clothing that hinders your movement (for example, don't wear pants that are so tight you are wondering if they will burst at the seams when you sit down. Don't wear clothes that are so baggy or long that you may trip on them or constantly be shuffling them)
*Wear appropriate shoes for the setting (don't wear high heels or painful shoes when you might take a walking tour of a large facility)
*Avoid colors that are too bright or busy with patterns (they can be a distraction)
*Make sure bags and briefcases are professional and easy to carry (backpacks falling off the shoulder or open purses that may spill if dropped are a bad idea)

2
ATTITUDE

I am sure that you have heard a variety of quotes about the importance of attitude. Many of them are dead on in the professional world; your attitude is vitally important to your job. Now sure, everyone is going to have a day where they, "just don't feel like doing x,y,z," but the way you react to that feeling is in your control.

Think back to a time that you have encountered a person, either co-worker or service person who had a negative attitude while working with you. I am sure you would agree that feelings of positivity and joy aren't exactly fluttering through your mind right now.

Honestly, those situations leave lasting impressions and change our views about people and our interactions with the world. It is up to us as individuals to make a choice to add to the ugliness or step out and be different. Our world has an abundance of negativity, let's change that.

Part of creating and maintaining a good reputation means that you must carry yourself in a way that demonstrates reliability, class, responsiveness, positivity, and a good work ethic. There will be times when you are required to lead and times when you will be required to follow. There is no way to know when those times will come, but if you are a solidly well rounded professional you will be prepared for any situation.

The more that you are able to show an attitude of professionalism, the more you will be trusted and relied upon. At times, this will be very beneficial for career growth opportunities. Shine a positive light on yourself.

Attitude Adjustments
*Be respectful to anyone and everyone you come across
*Be punctual (respect the time of others as if it is your own)
*Show confidence in the way you carry yourself. Even if you do not feel confident, fake it 'till you make it
*Speak up! Your opinion and ideas matter. Be heard rather than being silent in the background
*Prioritize
*Set goals
*Be bold, try or suggest new things (if you can support why it is a good idea)
*Be positive and encouraging, try to find the good in every situation
*Stay calm under pressure
*Maintain a good reputation by being honest
*Follow company rules and accept them for what they are
*Dress appropriately for the setting
*Have an attitude of leadership without micromanaging
*Give others the benefit of the doubt, we all make mistakes
*Smile
*Compliment others
*Help others in need, when you can
*Do not gossip, spread rumors, or bad mouth others
*Be trustworthy, keep confidential conversations to yourself
*Do your part by getting your job done to the best of your abilities
*Be willing to teach and share information with others
*Be prepared for your daily tasks, meetings, and presentations
*Be prepared to work independently or as a team player depending on the circumstance
*Volunteer

3
MANNERS

Who remembers this: "Did you say please?" "What do you say?" "Mind your manners." Many of us were taught the basic manners from the time we were little kids, wiping our noses with our sleeves. However, at times we may become a bit lazy with our basic manners.

Perhaps around friends we speak a bit more loosely or use more slang. For example, we may change the most basic of manners to something "simpler," such as saying thanks instead of thank you. When squeezing by someone we may just "try to make it" and apologize if there is a negative outcome, instead of saying "Excuse me" up front. In a professional environment, basic manners will go a long way.

More and more, when I am out and about I come across people who are amazed by good manners. At one point I worked at a preschool and I dedicated thirty days to work on manners. My aide, a seventy year old woman named Margaret, loved the children, but after years of teaching, her favorite phrase was, "they are all just a bunch of pills now, no manners, no respect." To say the least, she was thrilled about the curriculum I created for the children and we were both excited about the change.

You may be thinking, well that sounds fantastic, Lisa, but I am not a kid. After all, isn't this a book about professionalism? Absolutely. A large part of presenting a professional attitude has more to do with the basics than we might think. Sometimes going back to the ABC's of life helps us get a refresher and helps us look at habits we may have developed over time.

Out with some of the new, in with some of the old?

*Acknowledge people! (Ignoring people, regardless of our mood is flat out rude)

*Greet people formally (hello vs. hey)

*Hold the door open for people

*Just say "please" (no matter how old the relationship, people feel good about receiving requests vs. demands)

*Just as important, just say "thank you" (gratitude makes others feel helpful and there is nothing wrong with spreading "joyful" feelings to others)

*Say "excuse me" when you are trying to get by or if you have a bodily function mishap

*See someone in need? Give them a hand (we will all need help at some point or another);

*Make eye contact in conversations (this shows the person you are engaged and listening)

*Be courteous of people's time be being punctual

*Be conscientious of people's body language (if they seem to be in a hurry to leave, respect that and help out by not telling them about your cat's recent surgery)

*Carry conversations out of the stream of traffic, not everyone is in a position to chat casually

*Do not interrupt (be kind in hearing others out)

*Include others in a conversation if they arrive on the scene (no one likes to feel like the odd man out)

*Cover your mouth when you cough, sneeze, or burp (people are unaware if you are ill or just had a tickle in your throat)

*Respect people's personal space (some people do not appreciate the shoulder pat or being close enough to smell our breath)

*If sharing space, be respectful of each other's space

4
COMMUNICATION

Have you ever had that moment where you call a business and the person on the other end sounded like you just completely interrupted them? This has happened to many of us, and we may have even wondered if they could hear themselves. There are some moments that I believe people are completely unaware of their "telephone voice." I learned very early on in my life that a person can "hear your smile" over the phone. Just as someone can hear a smile, there is a variety of information they can hear. The sound of irritation, joy, hurriedness, or sadness are easily recognizable over the phone by most people.

Tone over the phone is no longer the only aspect of communication In this day of technology, phone communication has grown to include e-mail, social media, and text messages. These forms of communication can be a danger in the professional world. Whether a message went to the wrong person, a message was misinterpreted, or an e-mail contained restricted information, communication must be handled carefully.

I am not trying to make you paranoid, just aware. Professionally, communication typically travels at a rapid pace whether that is over the phone or in passing in the hall. So many of us are caught in a state of business that we may not be as cautious as we should.

Whether we are using a landline or a cell phone, proper etiquette still applies.

Please silence your cell phones now

*When possible, silence your phone during meetings or when working with others

*Let the caller hear the smile in your voice

*Speak clearly and at a reasonable sound level

*Greet the caller with a "Good morning/afternoon" and your name

*Continue to use the same manners that you would in person

*If a caller is angry, stay calm and acknowledge their concerns

*Listen to a caller's request before answering the question

*If another line rings, ask the caller to hold long enough to put the next caller on hold, then return to the first call

*Keep personal calls to a minimum during your work day

*If you are unable to answer the caller's questions, get the needed information and get back to them. Simply saying "I don't know," is not professional

*Personal ring tones in professional environments should not consist of possible offensive lyrics or crude humor

*End each call with asking whether or not the caller is in need of any further information

*When speaking to supervisors over the phone, do not hesitate to meet in person if there is a complex situation

*When answering and hanging up the phone, keep background noise (such as music or conversations) to a minimum

*Do not pick up the phone when speaking to someone else, give the caller your undivided attention

*If you need to take a message or call the person at a later time, write down the date, time of call, name and phone number (repeat the number back for verification)

5
ORGANIZATION

Whether you are sharing an office, a cubicle, or not sharing at all, organization is essential for a professional environment. Being organized can help keep work at a manageable level, keep priorities in order, track deadlines and appointments, as well as provide mental peace for ourselves.

We all have different habits and work styles, but cluttered space has the tendency to make people feel overwhelmed. Picture this: you got the job and even obtained the corner office, your supervisor walks you over and half way opens the door, revealing a room filled with clutter nearly to the ceiling. The supervisor says, "it's all yours if you clear it out." Most of us immediately feel overwhelmed, and we may say to ourselves, "this is a mess and I have no idea where to start or where to put things." Then we stand back, take a deep breath and start the process.

If we keep our space organized, we can potentially avoid the feeling of being overwhelmed. Organization can make our work day easier. I can hear some of you saying, "I can find my stuff in my messes just fine." I don't doubt that, I am merely suggesting trying something new to help ourselves.

At one point, I was professionally organizing homes, and hands down the biggest reason for the clutter was, "I just don't know how." For some this was a generational "tradition," for others it was due to time constraints. Here are some easy and practical tips for organizing your space professionally.

Everything has a place

*Arrange furniture according to your work style (if you frequently use the right side of the desk for writing, account for that when arranging)

*Do not place infrequently used items on the desktop

*Use organizational supplies, such as "inbox bins" to keep paperwork in order

*Use folders (or whatever else works for you) to separate daily to-do's from ongoing projects

*If possible, use electronic calendars and sticky notes to track work rather than having extra clutter on your desk

*If necessary, create a notebook or binder that you use for stray notes rather than cluttering the wall or bulletin board with reminders

*Keep small items such as paperclips or tacks in separate containers or a drawer organizer

*Keep trinkets and personal items to a minimum to avoid clutter

*Have a designated area for your briefcase or personal belongings (a hidden spot is better if possible, such as in a drawer or under the desk)

*Hang your coat or sweater on a coatrack or hook rather than hanging it on your chair

*Use the last few minutes of the day to reorganize your desk for your return

*Bundle your computer and phone cables with tie straps, or other items that will help them appear neat

*Push in your chair when you are away from your desk

*Use file cabinets and folders for organizing paperwork, organize the drawers according to how frequently you use them, in alphabetical order or use color-coding

*Keep snacks and food out of sight

*At the end of each week, dust your space (computer, phone, desk) completely

6
KNOWLEDGE

When I was an Office Manager some years ago, we decided to hire a high school student looking for their first job. The owner and I were very well aware that we were helping to build a foundation for this girl's future employment and we were determined to do the best we could. During her interview, I asked her what she was most interested in learning, and she smiled and said how to do a good job and work hard. I was immediately excited about her goals.

However, I started to ask, what does it truly mean to do a good job? Part of doing a good job in a professional or any other environment means that you have to exercise a level of dedication and commitment to learning your job. Seems obvious right? Let's take a harder look at that, though. If we asked ourselves right now how well we knew our job, what would the response be? Personally, I believe there is always room for growth in learning.

The amount of learning that we do is completely up to us. Our results are based on the effort that we put in. We cannot expect top notch results with little to no effort. Learning is a lifelong process. It is limitless. We live in a world filled with information at our fingertips. Information is accessible anywhere at any time. We can choose to access the information available to us. The key is whether or not we will seek the information needed and put it into action. At times, answers may come easy, and voila, problem solved. Other times, searching for answers could go on for a lifetime.

Seek, find, do

*Familiarize yourself with your company's policies, rules, and regulations
*Ask questions of senior staff
*Use the internet, after all, what can't be found online?
*Visit your local library or bookstore and read up on specific topics
*Look up words you do not know, how else will you know what they mean?
*Network with others in the same field
*Take notes about topics that you are unsure of
*Research using reliable sources in order to become confident in what you learn
*Volunteer for opportunities that seem challenging to you
*Seek training in your career field
*Be willing to spend some of your own time learning about your work
*Subscribe to podcasts, audiobooks, or video channels
*Teach someone something you know, this will sharpen your own skills
*Enroll in online or live courses
*Use visual items such as maps or drawings that give you a better understanding of the topic
*Draw or doodle out your questions and thoughts on a topic
*Journal or outline to help you sort out concepts
*Take a field trip (i.e. if you work in a scientific field go to a science museum)
*Read and quiz yourself on the material you read
*Sleep well and exercise regularly to get the most of your brain power
*Play old fashioned board games with a spin (i.e. if you are a manager, play scrabble only creating management words)

7
WRITING

I remember hearing some years ago that writing has gone out of style, with all that technology has to offer. Perhaps it is true that we have traded traditional pen and paper for a keyboard and a screen. Nothing is wrong with changing with the times, but one thing has not changed: professionals need to be able to communicate clearly and formally through writing.

Regardless if the writing comes in the form of a message, memo, e-mail, or letter, the contents need to be communicated correctly. Let's take a look at the statements below:

"Please stop by my office today, we need to discuss something."

"Stop by my office today, WE need to discuss something!"

Word usage, capital letters, and punctuation can cause the reader to interpret messages differently. One may be seen as threatening or intimidating, while the other just may peak curiosity. What we read and interpret causes emotional reactions, and we may not always "read into" things correctly.

Help your reader understand the point you are making by choosing your words and phrases carefully. Speak clearly through your words without giving too little or too much detail. Make your point while avoiding repetition or incomplete thoughts. Here are some simple ideas to help you cross those t's and dot those i's, whether by hand or through typing.

Word power

*Do not limit your vocabulary, use a thesaurus

*If you are unsure of the meaning of a word, spare yourself embarrassment by looking it up

*Always include a relevant subject line

*Always include a date

*Avoid use of all capital letters as it appears CONFRONTATIONAL

*Use blue and black ink on important or formal documents (save your favorite orange pen for your personal notes)

*Always include return addresses or your contact information

*Remember words can be misinterpreted because the reader can't see you, so choose your words carefully

*Always start and end on a positive note even if difficult issues need to be addressed

*Understand the lingo of your company and use it when appropriate

*Give credit where credit is due, add the recipient's professional title to their name (i.e. Dr. Jones)

*Use easy to read fonts

*Avoid colored fonts on formal e-mails

*Use correct punctuation

*Be concise, avoid filler words and phrases

*Avoid abbreviations and contractions in formal writing

*Be careful with predictive text or spell checking corrections

*Choose the right homonym (i.e. affect/effect, site/cite/sight, to/too/two)

*Formatting is important, evaluate the way your document looks

*Do not use slang

* Write out numerals (thirty vs. 30)

*Watch out for repetition

8
CO-WORKERS

As you undoubtedly already know, the world is filled with various personalities. The workplace is no different. Many of us have had the co-worker that is our sidekick and ultra-reliable, and more than likely also had the co-worker who, unbeknownst to them, is more helpful when absent than when working beside us. Life is constantly changing, and that happens in work environments, too. People come and people go.

Our goal is to focus on the person we can change: **ourselves**. How we interact with our co-workers can lead to joyful environments or rotten ones. First thing first, accept the fact that you are not in control of others. If Dottie wants to paint her nails, or Rob wants to play solitaire all day, the question is how can you maintain your professionalism in a less than ideal environment?

Encountering individuals who are hard workers, team players, go-getters, or not is inevitable. If you can be consistent in your actions, behaviors, and interactions, the better off you will be. You must be prepared though, some workplaces can be a lot like high school. People do not always say the kindest things; you may be called a kiss up or worse. Accept that possibility and do your job. Focus on what your priorities and tasks are, and remind yourself why you are there.

Take pride in the professional that you are, work hard, bring positivity to the office, take the high road when you can. When there is a mix of personalities there will be contentious moments. How will you handle those moments while maintaining a professional attitude?

Only the high road

*Always greet your coworkers regardless of your personal feelings toward them

*Complete your tasks to the best of your ability even if others are not

*Avoid gossip, back biting, and water cooler talk about others

*If engaged in one of the above topics, simply advise that they should talk to the person directly

*Salary information should be kept confidential

*Be accountable for your actions, do not ask coworkers to "cover for you"

*Take responsibility for the good and the bad regarding your performance, do not blame others

*Do not "cover for" others, you are not responsible for their actions

*Reserve personal conversations for your breaks outside of the office or after hours

*Be polite, kind, and considerate of the feelings of others

*Be willing to help when you are able

*Be encouraging, positive, and offer uplifting perspectives in times of difficulty

*Do not engage in activities against company policy

*Avoid language and discussion of topics that potentially can be offensive

*Avoid crude jokes and conversations with sexual undertones

*Respect the space and property of others

*Ask permission to borrow belongings of others rather than assuming "they won't mind"

*Avoid discussions regarding religion, politics, or personal beliefs when possible

*Show a little bit of grace, we all have bad days or moments, be understanding

9
MANAGING TIME

When I think about extended families, I have heard stories very similar to these: "Tell Aunt Edna the party starts an hour earlier, because she is never on time," "We need to get going, we are on a schedule!" or, "don't rush me, I am on vacation." All of these ideas, whether they happen in your family or not, revolve around time. How a person chooses to manage their time will vary greatly. In a professional environment, the same thought applies.

I have had co-workers who had to be the first to arrive, last to leave, and all tasks had to be done. Other co-workers were last to arrive, first to leave, and no tasks were done. I encourage you to be a well-balanced professional, and spend your time wisely. Here is a snapshot of a day that would be a possible "balanced" option between work and home:

5:00am-7:20am: Wake up, get ready, prior to leaving the house take care of personal to-do's
7:45am: Arrive at work: Check/respond to e-mails, messages, to-do list, and look over calendar
8:00-11:55am: Work and meetings
11:55am-12:00pm: Tidy up desk, add to to-do list
12:00pm-1:00pm: Lunch-catch up on personal to-do's including e-mails, messages, and calls
1:00pm-4:45pm: Work and meetings
4:45pm-5:00pm: Tidy up area, work on to-do list for following day
5:00pm: Go home and spend time with family

This exact schedule may not work for everyone, but routines and habits will help each one of us long term.

Tick Tock, Tick Tock

*Start your work day 15 minutes earlier (review messages, e-mail and your calendar)
*Prioritize your tasks according to the earliest deadline
*Schedule your day by using your calendar
*Keep personal phone calls to a minimum
*Review text messages and personal e-mails during your break
*Learn what your distractions are and remove them while working
*Keep conversations unrelated to work to a minimum unless you are on a break
*Delegate when you are able
*Use a to-do list
*Know when to say no, if you are too busy do not accept an extra task if you cannot manage it
*Do not take breaks longer than allowable
*Do not procrastinate, get the work done
*Have a backup plan if a task takes longer than expected
*Set daily, weekly, and monthly goals
*Take a few minutes to reorganize your desk before lunch
*Give time to the important things, rather than to unimportant things
*Consider focusing on one task rather than multiple tasks as switching tasks can cause your concentration to break
*Complete the most difficult tasks first
*Self-motivate
*Develop routines and habits
*Get plenty of rest so that you are not slowed down by tiredness
*Exercise to help clear your mind
*If you need help, ask rather than worry and overanalyze
*Practice speed reading

10
YOUR MOMENT

Say nice things to yourself on a daily basis as you become the professional person you want to be.
Tell yourself:

I am a professional.

I have greatness to contribute to my environment.

I will approach my new job as if I am a child experiencing something great for the first time.

I can and will be disciplined.

I can and will be on time.

I can and will live an organized life.

I will be confident, even under pressure.

I will approach things with the patience of an older, more mature adult.

I will be understanding and kind because we all have different life experiences.

I am brave enough to volunteer for opportunities even if they seem like a challenge.

I will seek answers, I will become informed, and I will act.

I will be a good example to future employees.

I will not gossip, but I will always offer words of kindness and encouragement.

I will avoid distractions and stay focused.

I will always treat others will respect.

I have the ability to lead or follow when necessary.

I can accept when I am wrong and admit it.

I do not have to follow the behaviors of those around me.

I have to live with a thirst for learning so that I can mature confidently.

I have goals that need to be met, and I will meet them.

I will get enough rest, eat healthy and exercise so that I can feel better about myself.

I will ask questions, I will take notes, and I will work hard even when my tasks are difficult.

I am determined to shine.

The more professional I am, the greater my opportunities become.

I will dress modestly to display respect for myself and others.

My ideas matter, I will speak up and make them known.

I am a confidently maturing professional.

ABOUT THE AUTHOR

Lisa Bracy currently lives in Northern New Mexico, with her husband, three children and lots of pets. When she is not busy as a professional full time employee, she loves to read and write books, work on business ventures and learn. She has a passion for helping others develop and grow with confidence. Her goal for each of her books is for every reader to understand the importance of learning to be a better person. In doing so we can all share a bit of greatness with the world and make a difference in the lives of others.

www.ingramcontent.com/pod-product-compliance
Lightning Source LLC
Chambersburg PA
CBHW060559030426
42337CB00019B/3577